THE ART OF HEALTH COACHING

THE ART OF HEALTH COACHING

AVERY NIGHTINGALE

CONTENTS

CHAPTER 1

Introduction to Health Coaching

Health coaching is a window into an individual's lifestyle and how they experience life. Over 80% of health conditions are connected to lifestyle, and the good news is that we can significantly impact our health and well-being with simple habit changes. The purpose of health coaching is to guide and support clients, helping them reach their most functional state. According to the National Consortium for Credentialing Health and Wellness Coaches (NC-CHWC), "a health & wellness coach is a professional who helps people assess their current physical and emotional state and helps them set goals and develop a plan to achieve and maintain optimal health."

This approach aligns with the philosophies of Chiropractic and Holistic health, connecting body structure and body function. It recognizes that the mind, body, and spirit are intertwined, and knowledge is the first step in reaching a new level of health. This month, we wanted to share with you the guide to our health coaching training, authored by NP Suit, BSN, RN, DC, herself a health coach. This series of articles will help you refine your current health and wellness expertise into a new level of care; truly masterful coaching.

We'll start with "The 11 Principles of Health Coaching"—where you will learn the focus of coaching in great detail—and then move toward information for patients gained through The Behavior Change Science Basic Training for the ultimate self-care.

Defining Health Coaching

You are about to enter a learning space designed to take your understanding of yourself, your clients, and the interconnections that define them to a deeper level. A new type of curriculum that will shine a spotlight on tiny nuances and complex layers that often "fly under the radar." A leading-edge coaching approach that takes a multi-dimensional perspective—pulling from the inner-most consciousness of personal change and from positive psychology, mind-body medicine, and wellness—to help clients create solutions that really, truly fit them. Welcome to the world of health coaching—getting under the problem to the solution.

Before we begin, it's helpful to share a common understanding of what health coaching actually is. Health coaching is a relatively recent addition to the healthcare system, acting as a preventive, holistic, and patient-centered approach that encompasses not only lifestyle and behavior but also all forms of wellness and complementary/alternative medicine. Health coaching emphasizes realistic goal setting and accountability for taking care of oneself, even for those facing chronic and acute mental or physical health challenges. It is distinct from both wellness coaching and health education. Health coaching is designed to offer clients accountability, lifestyle counseling, problem-solving, stress management, spiritual and emotional wellness, and exercise prescriptions. Because health coaching is an educational approach—which avoids giving advice or solving problems—on realistic goal setting and solution-focused skills, coaches and clients use their hours of telephone time to discuss wellness-related solutions, while also building a line of communication between visits to their healthcare providers.

Importance of Health Coaching in Wellness

Health coaching has become a popular tool for reaching and exceeding wellness goals. It meets people where they are to develop and refine their own personalized approaches. Coaching is the art of using communication, conversations, and behavior change to impact health and wellness. It is important to note the distinction between a coaching mentality and coaching tactics. Yes, stacking coaching tactics like the Stages of Change model or Motivational Interviewing into what you already offer for your wellness clients will make your programs or services more effective. It's just as, if not more, important to integrate an overarching "coach approach" mental shift.

What good is increasing your client's lung capacity by 20%, their chiropractic status by 50%, or decreasing their BMI by 35% if they're still addicted to food as a comfort? Even if they manage to keep their weight off, they're still not getting the same excitement out of their lives as someone who is more intrinsically food-moderate. Their wellness isn't as high. Their health isn't as high. It's not necessarily the wellness program's fault. If we really want full and vital wellness, we need to incorporate coaching. People with the best wellness tend to use what I call a coaching "mentality." What this means is that they are making choices about working on the inside as well as on the outside. They are taking a big-picture approach to wellness. Coaching provides people with focus on actual well-being and quality of life, as well as the transitional goal of cultivating healthy habits.

CHAPTER 2

Foundations of Wellness Expertise

One of the most important aspects of health coaching is to be knowledgeable about the human body. We can all relate that when something doesn't feel right, when sickness is involved, or there is a step toward wellness needing to take place, the human body is capable of producing the most discomfort in our lives. Wellness is also about potential and not just disease avoidance, which, in facility-based settings, can often become a monotonous dialogue. Regardless of what we think wellness is as health coaches, the constant among us is that our physical body responds in a particular way to recommendations, coaching, and influences on our health. The human body is the one body of knowledge that pulls us all into agreement about what the subject of wellness really is. We all have a working model of the human body and its associated systems, reactions, what illness is, what causes it, and what the cures might be. The very deep physiology, however, is not what most of us are experts in. Rather, it's knowledge of how to purposefully manage the systems that keep the body healthy.

To know and understand what health can be, it is important for health coaches to be able to answer some key questions about employers, consumers, and future audiences, the material of which is no less than the human body. Key questions which will be addressed and laid out will include strategies to the body's homeostatic processes; how the body manages outside threats and how to aid this process; how it reacts to the intake of dietary materials; what it does with those materials after it uses them; how the body rests; fundamental principles of nutrition; and basic dietary habits cultivated for human civilizations.

Understanding Human Anatomy and Physiology

Refining your wellness expertise: The art of health coaching involves understanding human anatomy and physiology. I tend to appreciate people like health coaches when they have a few more letters behind their name, indicating a college degree. People need to be prepared to offer me advice. They need to understand the structures and processes of the body and what factors influence those structures and processes. There is no secret about my body and its health. Any health coach who offers me advice knows that digestion and absorption are two processes involved in the body's use of food. The nutritional community is a breakthrough. In many situations, there is a need for nutrients across all metabolic processes. Although inflammation is a part of certain metabolic processes going really wrong, other nutrients are always important. Antioxidants, being a part of natural materials and a part of the food category from plants, gather information on other roles developed as humankind became educated about natural and scientifically supported nutrient interrelationships. If your attitude is to isolate the antioxidant from the plant and the system it helps support, then you are a likely user of the nutrients I like to label as bystanders.

Bystander nutrients are nutrients that have little or no chance of doing harm, even in high doses. To make this point clear, vitamin E can lessen high-density lipoprotein cholesterol, also known as HDL or "happy" cholesterol, if taken in high doses. In lower doses, however, vitamin E can act as an antioxidant and protect HDL cholesterol. These "bystanders" hold doors open; they do not choose a path at all. I like health coaches who want to find their own path, specialize in a health-related niche, and advise on things important to them, their families, and their friends, not because of the greatest financial potential, but because understanding in the area is what you give to the world. Specialize in building a busy practice utilizing this valuable information.

Nutrition and Diet Fundamentals

Have you ever had a client in nutrition coaching who you are confident could get a stronger command of the role of good, healthy food for health? I have mentioned how important it is to maintain optimal nutrition, which goes beyond vitamins and individuals rethinking whether or not to take dietary supplements. Good nutrition comes from eating brilliantly nutritious, unprocessed food.

Diet is crucial. This one fits today's health team so well that we are well-positioned to help our customers recognize how healthful eating will help them avoid food-related health problems before needing our colleagues in the healthcare community to patch them up from conditions too much diet may trigger. In "The 4 Foods Fixes" article, I address clients' need to take control of their own well-being and talk about the effect that research has shown consuming diabetic food eaters. I assume most of our customers are in the later category, either suffering from issues today or worried about getting them in the future. That's never to suggest that food options don't bring impact on the everyday experience and how our customers feel about themselves today. In most cases, no one really wants to wait a decade to find out a degree of correlation. To be honest, sticking to an indulgent diet high in sugar and trans fat can rob energy, cause depression, and affect human illness by not already having enough reserves of carefully picked nutrients and by overloading the machine of people with fraudulent food. Aside from the question of whether poor nutrition is terrible science or poor practice, it's definitely not a perfect way to do wellness or avoid health risks. To do that, we are forced to set up and manage good, nutrient-dense eating habits.

Specialize in building a busy practice utilizing this valuable information.

CHAPTER 3

Communication and Relationship Building

Health coaching is a unique and fascinating combination of professional skills. As a health coach, you can impart decades of knowledge in mere minutes. Your honesty and commitment to serve will help place the stranger at the opposite side of your screen at ease. You echo back the important pieces of the story your client shares, reflecting and validating each point in turn. Your client may feel heard, understood, and appreciated for their inner wisdom. If you've been noticed, you've already made a good start with this stranger on their wellness path. You now have the raw material needed to help shape the individual's plan for living their best life.

Active Listening

Active listening is a skill set that has been refined and focused into communication. Listening is like a waterfall, the basics of everything. The entire coaching process revolves around client-centered listening. As you listen, your questions may be answered, but do not dive in just yet. Likewise, do not jump to solutions in your mind or allow your facial expression to reveal your skepticism or overenthusiasm. Even in writing, empathy seeps through. Empathy, which is different from sympathy, is both an emotional and intellectual connection. Lots of people think they are empathic when what they are really doing is projecting their own experience onto another person. Sympathy is when we feel what the other person is feeling; empathy is when we understand the emotional and intellectual dimensions of their story. Our cared-for being can sense that we understand them top to bottom, start to finish, chapter and verse. Make every word and action resonate that you're all ears.

Building Relationships Based Upon Trust

When individuals feel validated, heard, and empathized with, the bond is strengthened. A professional relationship has been established. By meeting our clients where they are, they are inspired to trust us. Remember, trust cannot be established overnight.

Active Listening Skills

The ability to listen is an essential skill for a health coach. It is our core endeavor to fully comprehend a client's concerns by listening to verbal language, tone of voice, diction, and other nonverbal cues. When a coach demonstrates that they are paying close attention to what the client is saying with their full focus on the topic and individual, the client forms an initial impression, ultimately fostering an open dialogue of trust. When talking to our clients about goals and motivation, it is essential that a coach be genuinely present in conversation. A great way to show one is actively listening is by occasionally repeating or rephrasing an aspect of what the client is saying but in a more concise manner. It's also beneficial to continually offer feedback and ask for questions and/or clarification, knowing when to inquire about the future or potential problems. If a client raises personal concerns, emotions, or hidden preoccupations, a coach with great active listening skills can provide comfort, guidance, and empathy rather than superficial advice or opinions.

For example, a client may not like the outcome of a particular training program because the routine does not include exercises aimed at building muscle mass. His only view was to improve his body sculpting by reducing body fat. In this scenario, a good coach would never diminish the possible concerns of the client's desire to build muscle mass by merely noting "you don't really need to." Instead, a health coach with exceptional active listening skills would show empathy and sound encouragement by saying "It sounds like you take a lot of pride in your lean muscle mass, and maintaining that could be something really good to focus on in the meantime as you start the new program." This demonstrates the coach is both fully attentive and responsive to the client's wants and needs while still addressing the issue at hand.

Empathy and Emotional Intelligence

Empathy has a dazzling definition in its grandiloquent form. It is the ability to sense others' feelings and to take an active interest in their perspective. Simple, right? It means that when someone comes to us, we are effectively able to discern what is going on inside their bodies and hearts, and articulate their experiences in words. In other words, we are able to enter their shoes and identify with them.

Emotional intelligence refers to our ability to process information, relate, interact, and solve problems in the emotional realm. To break this down into its simplest terminology, the following components of emotional intelligence are identified:

- The awareness of your own emotions and the ability to manage them.
- Demonstrating empathy.
- Developing clear and precise interaction with others.
- Applying social skills to build relationships and networks.

The goal of reaching a preliminary understanding and developing an empathic relationship with a coachee (newcomer) or patient is to provide a condition in which advice and leadership can be customized to the coachee's behavior and struggles, and the patient's self-confidence as the relationship matures might increase. It relates to understanding the world of the client/patient, their state of mind, the accompanying feelings, what motivates or worries them, and what discourages or frightens them.

CHAPTER 4

Behavior Change Techniques

To gain a broad understanding of coaching as a health profession, it is necessary to become familiar with various behavior change techniques commonly used. Some of the most common techniques include goal setting, problem-solving, active listening, and the use of motivational interviewing. Health coaching occurs in the context of the motivation for change that the client brings with them. When a client is highly motivated to change, it typically only requires a bit of advice. However, when a client is preparing to make a change, a clear decision is needed, along with more information, support, and guidance to examine options and the effects of that change through problem analysis.

Health coaches typically switch to and utilize motivational interviewing, active listening, goal setting, and problem-solving skills to help elicit change talk and strengthen the client's intrinsic motivation. Motivational interviewing is a beautiful technique that any therapist worth their salt should be utilizing to increase intrinsic motivation and help the client with outcome setting. Healthcare providers also use motivational interviewing techniques to help elicit change talk and strengthen the patient's intrinsic motivation for change. Goal setting and action planning are key to interdisciplinary and/or intradisciplinary provider-client coordination for improved self-monitoring of the client's adherence to managed behavioral change.

Motivational Interviewing

The second strategy of the OARS skill set focuses on affirmations. Affirmations are a key behavior change strategy, and research has shown that they can positively impact conversations. It is also recommended in the Motivational Interviewing theory. The act of providing affirmations shows appreciation for the client, presents positive feedback, and structures the conversation to allow the client to expand on the affirmative remark. This section looks at what affirmations are, how they are utilized, the principles of affirmative language, and the application of using affirmations within a health coaching conversation.

Motivational Interviewing, a widely accepted health coaching technique, consists of four key principles: engage, focus, evoke, and plan. These steps work towards supporting an individual through the process of change. Motivational Interviewing is a counseling method designed to help individuals find the internal motivation they need to change their lives for the better. It focuses on personal values and implications, and counseling and resources are fundamental, things that traditional methods lack. Motivational Interviewing creates a scenario where the person believes they are making the decision, when in fact the healthcare worker is guiding them with thoughtful, open questions. It uses a pain management approach that centers on "What are you going to do in those moments when it's difficult to take the next right step?" This patient-centered approach using affirmations works very well in the health coaching model. With an affirming approach, one would expect to see a client/patient-centered conversation, all treatment and non-treatment choices to be addressed, and how best to support clients to ensure that health is maintained.

Motivational interviewing is based on the technique of listening to what the client is saying. A coach does not give solutions; they remain neutral and create a nonjudgmental job, ensuring the patient/client is heard without being lectured. The coach asks basic questions to clarify what the patient/client needs/does not want, why the changes are important to them (not the coach), and what the client is willing and able to do to change.

Goal Setting and Action Planning

Goal setting is one of the most important aspects of an effective coaching relationship. Research shows that effective goal setting can increase the client's motivation to change. Aim to collaboratively set specific, measurable, achievable, relevant, and time-constrained (SMART) goals with your client. A SMART goal is a clearly stated outcome that can be reached in a specific time frame. When setting SMART goals, you will focus on what the client wants to improve. In doing so, consider the following questions:

- What outcome is important to you?
- What does it look like?
- How will you know when it is reached?
- What are your first steps?
- What else could you do?
- What action would be easiest to do?

Consider potential barriers within the coaching and engagement process. Goal setting has long been an essential component of behavior change interventions, and recent research confirms its essential role. In one study, participants presented with a difficulty-rated changing goal were significantly more likely to move forward within a week (61%) or even within two weeks (83%). When a clearly stated intention to meet a healthy goal is expressed, progress toward that goal becomes much more attainable.

After ensuring the goal is both feasible and compelling, the client needs to verbalize it in the affirmative tense. If the individual does not appreciate the goal at an intuitive level, then the change effort will likely fail or, at a minimum, not evolve. It is essential to get clarity on three to five of these issues to help motivate the client and link back to other goals.

CHAPTER 5

Ethical and Legal Considerations in Health Coachin

Ethical and legal considerations are crucial aspects of health coaching, as they impact clients, the health coach, and potentially other health professionals. Health and wellness coaches should be committed to adhering to the standards of the profession to earn common respect. As a coach, remember that no one expects you to be a counselor, therapist, or personal trainer. However, you do need to understand potential ethical and legal hot spots well enough to know what you can and should do in those situations, as well as when to refer a client to professionals in other domains.

Ethical considerations are informed by your professional association's ethical guidelines, as well as by principles of flexibility, client autonomy, and prevailing legal guidelines. Legal aspects involve the laws of a locality or country and ensuring compliance with them.

The five hallmarks of professionalism discussed earlier (personal conduct, third-party support, custom programming, scope of practice, and referral) can help a health coach frame these difficult issues for themselves and begin to identify the best way to approach them. It is important for the coach to take reasonable precautions to protect or guard confidential information obtained through coaching relationships. It is expected that fitness professionals will do their utmost to maintain the privacy and respect the confidentiality of client and member information.

To be brought to a level, determine what is legally mandatory in a state or country. Beyond that, coaches may require their clients to fill out waivers allowing them to communicate with other health professionals if a medical emergency arises. This is a subtle but important point: when a deemed or apparent emergency arises, the coach does not have to tell the health professional anything. The coach may simply call an ambulance or take the client to the emergency room.

Understanding and navigating these ethical and legal considerations ensure that health coaches can provide safe, respectful, and effective guidance to their clients.

CHAPTER 6

Cultural Competence and Diversity Awareness

Transcultural and cultural competence are terms that have been used to describe healthcare systems and the services offered within a facility. In contrast, cultural competence is an ongoing developmental journey that many people are still engaged in. It includes goals and aspirations but allows for constancy, refocusing, and change.

Educating oneself about cultural diversity, fidelity, and the adoption of cultural humility can help remove the pressure associated with striving to be competent in the face of a constantly changing environment. This education can help clarify individual values, assumptions, biases, unexpected terminology, and unanticipated responses. Being aware of cultural differences as varying belief systems and ways of adapting to wellness, well-being, and health is essential when tailoring a health coaching plan for each individual.

The experience of health, wellness, and well-being is profoundly influenced by culture and social relationships. Being diverse-aware will help uncover racist, sexist, ethnocentric, ageist, and ableist cultural attitudes, which can be barriers to counseling effectively across cultures. Specializing in diversity is indispensable and a liability if the health service provider lacks this understanding. It is essential that it be a priority for all providers of healthcare.

In the environment of health coaching, attentive acknowledgment of diverse racial and ethnic portrayals is required in publications, teaching and instruction resources, and involvement approaches. It is important to try to choose students who are diverse and willing to offer their insights as an underrepresented community. Educating oneself about cultural diversity and fidelity, and adopting cultural humility, may help remove the pressure associated with striving to be competent in the face of the relentless changing environment. Educating oneself can help clarify individual values, assumptions, and biases, unexpected terminology, and unanticipated responses.

Cultural competence includes understanding that wellness and health experiences vary significantly across different cultural and social contexts. It helps to create more effective health coaching strategies that respect these differences and tailor approaches to meet diverse needs.

Ultimately, the goal is to foster an inclusive environment that respects and values the diverse backgrounds and perspectives of all individuals. This commitment to cultural competence and diversity awareness is not just about being considerate; it's about being effective in helping individuals achieve their best health and wellness outcomes.

CHAPTER 7

Advanced Coaching Strategies

In this session, our focus is on several advanced coaching strategies. From a positive psychology perspective, the first strategy we'll consider is the use of appreciative inquiry. Appreciative inquiry is based on the belief that organizations, like the people in them, have far greater potential than often realized. From this perspective, we reframe our questions and our perspectives to focus on our positive capabilities and possibilities for growth. This feeds directly into strengths-based coaching.

Strengths-based coaching emphasizes an explicit focus on capitalizing on what is right and building on strengths first. We're all familiar with coaching, but are we practiced with some of these advanced coaching strategies? Do we embody these ways of speaking and being? Many detractors of optimism abound in our society, attacking and removing the positive from our lives.

In response to negative influences, health coaches practicing advanced strategies often think, "I'm not going to regard that; I'm going to focus on the event and the moment." Several studies have shown that savoring the moment can lead to better health and improved life satisfaction.

Positive Psychology Principles

"The science of psychology should be focused on the study of human strengths rather than just illnesses." - Dr. Martin Seligman. Dissatisfaction with psychotherapists who looked solely for and treated pathology led to Dr. Martin Seligman's inaugural speech as the President of the American Psychological Association, where he unveiled this new science of positive psychology. Positive psychology shifts the healthcare focus, telling us that health and well-being do not necessarily reside in ridding patients of all that is wrong. It was time to turn toward studying what is right with people. To make such a shift within scientific disciplines practiced worldwide, the acceleration of positive psychology relied heavily on evidence-based science. Fortunately, the processes of positive psychology can be naturally integrated into coaching, as the spaces between traditional healthcare and coaching are already filled with shades of strengths.

The application of positive psychology in coaching isn't surprising. When interviewing nearly 400 member professionals at the International Coach Federation, Jayne Landeta found that an astonishing 83 percent of them spontaneously said that they focus on strengths when they coach. Positive psychology's evidence-based strategies are bursting with different content to support a strengths-based approach. In strengths-based coaching, people are encouraged to step outside the 'wall of their prison' to see their strengths and those of the people around them. This allows for resolving issues at hand using strengths to take control.

Strengths-Based Coaching

Gallup, Inc. has determined that the most integrated wellness programs and offerings are utilizing strengths-based tools and methodologies in their support to employees. This is exciting because health coaching tends to work from these same established strengths principles.

In this chapter, we will explore strengths-based coaching from a different perspective—focusing on strengths as virtues of character. This is more than just a different platform for supportive conversation. This chapter will teach you practical skills for engaging with the positive aspects of your clients, elevating them in their wellness goals and achievements. It brings the art of our health coach work to life.

This chapter is based on the VIA Institute's Classification of Character Strengths and Virtues. While there are many approved ways to categorize the full list of strengths into four, six, or twenty categories, positive psychology starts all discussions about strengths with the conversation around character strengths and virtues. We will do the same. That said, while the full list includes 24 character strengths, we will focus on a subset of those traditionally seen as particularly relevant to the process of wellness. The high road to the best life is in capitalizing on character strengths and gaining legitimate insight. Our work in well-being aligns almost seamlessly with character and values coaching as applied in the organizational realm. Coaching within this space empowers recipients and enhances self-efficacy by casting a spotlight on character strengths to grow from the inside out.

CHAPTER 8

Technology and Health Coaching

Technology in health coaching offers a more optimal setting for interventions, being touted as a game changer in delivering virtual coaching. Virtual coaching removes limits like geographic location, weather conditions, and driving distance, making it more convenient and ensuring continuity with less travel, absenteeism, and other sickness.

Sharp et al. describe telehealth as replacing videoconferencing health coaching to provide behavioral support. The range of apparent equipment items includes smartwatches, pedometers, and accelerometers that measure both activity and rest times. The use of technology and key features also encompasses calls. Various documents have been made available to help track software for wellness and healthcare coaches. Tracking software enables visualization and data creation to identify coaching areas and evaluate the effectiveness and return on investment of corporate wellness programs aimed at changing behavior.

Health coaching app usage implies that coaching technologies may improve participation and well-being. This trend continues to expand, with an estimated market size of $6.34 billion. The scope of coaching apps includes business, personal, and lifestyle areas, with Blue IQ integrated with different learning. Longo et al. researched how to validate evidence-based coaching apps. Global Industry Analysts highlight various health and well-being interoperable digital systems featuring performance measurement and behavior interfaces. Virtual coaching technologies extend beyond apps, including subscription plans that supplement in-person training. For example, virtual training provides a completely immersive experience outside physical facilities and is part of other wellness programs that have made a difference. Virtual training can provide business fitness centers with access to exercise-related knowledge, ongoing communication capabilities, and immediate direct contact with health experts, all expected to grow at a compound annual growth rate (CAGR) of 10.42%.

Digital Tools and Apps

Health coaches often utilize digital tools and apps as part of their approach to health coaching. Many, if not all, digital tools are created in cooperation with physical trainers, nutritionists, or other health coaches. There is a wide variety of free and professional digital tools in the market, each with unique features. Pay attention to the time and effort required to learn each tool proficiently and explore functions fundamental to a good client experience. However, the primary goal is to motivate clients to use technology in the long run. Most individuals searching for GPs and specialists are directed to digital tools by insurance websites. Using such tools, you can monitor your client's outcomes and advise them on assessing a digital tool if necessary.

Communication apps allow health coaches to give clients instant feedback through instant messaging, video calling, voice mails, and chat. Some wellness and health coaching centers maintain general-purpose social media accounts. Reliable email platforms (e.g., CRM software) enable you to change the brand to better represent your business and include specific options (e.g., in CRM marketing software, email automation messages). Electronic calendars are often used to schedule appointments and send email notifications to all parties involved. Many free personal training programs allow planning activities, checking exercises, and setting meetings for one person. However, paid training tip software is perfect for online trainers and wellness coaching companies, allowing health coaches to synchronize with electronic calendars, send and receive messages, and establish fitness standards.

Telehealth and Virtual Coaching

We are now in a modern health coaching age benefiting from technological advances that expand the parameters for effective wellness services. Health coaching can be further enhanced when coaches can provide their services anytime, anywhere. A recent consumer study indicated that getting health advice via the internet was the preferred method for many people. Telehealth and virtual coaching have the potential to extend the reach of individual health coaching to a larger percentage of the adult population, addressing many daily health issues and challenges.

Telecoaching is increasing globally. Face-to-face studies of physicians show a decline in coaching session demand, leading many to trust anonymous online services. Despite a personal need for face-to-face interaction, many prefer telehealth and virtual coaching due to trust issues and less face-to-face connection. This trend is forecasted to increase with the development of professional coaching platforms and credentialing bodies, along with enhanced communication reaching virtually coaching clients. Clients can see and evaluate wellness professionals for their fitness, Pilates, yoga, other training needs, and personal trainers, regardless of distance.

To solidify the movement of coaching coach-internet-based hardware and application programs such as Skype and FaceTime are used to meet wellness goals daily. Activities like cooking or walking with coaching help build clients' confidence and increase their desire for face-to-face coaching. This technology empowers health coaches to provide comprehensive and flexible support to their clients, ensuring a higher standard of care and improved outcomes.

CHAPTER 9

Evaluation and Assessment in Health Coaching

Effective health coaches must interpret and utilize evaluation and assessment data to help shape client enhancement. Evaluation and assessment in health coaching are multi-layered activities. At the macro level, tracking outcomes through annual changes in lifestyle, risk factors, and chronic disease progression provides an evidence-based method for assessing the impact of wellness programming. Within the one-on-one coaching session, tracking similar outcomes demonstrates evidence of change and a positive return on investment for the client, which may help increase their motivation to be a compliant participant.

One aspect of evaluation is understanding the different components of change and their likelihood of success. During the process of lifestyle and behavior coaching, often referred to as change management coaching, there are specific periods that form the sequence the client goes through—from being unaware of a potential need for change to the sustainment of new behaviors. This process is cyclical and broken down into four stages: precontemplation, contemplation, preparation, and action. Individuals are not likely to make progress through this cycle unless a significant event occurs to break the pattern of stagnation. Each stage represents essential elements of the client's readiness to make some form of change.

By assessing the client, the health coach is better able to use the coaching strategies and skills that are most likely to fit individual preferences for receiving feedback. This model also helps us to change our expectations and response to the client, moving away from a one-size-fits-all plan. Better results can be achieved using different strategies for different clients based on their coachability.

Evaluation Techniques

Health coaches should employ a variety of evaluation techniques to gather comprehensive data about their clients. These techniques may include surveys, interviews, physical assessments, and observational methods. By using a combination of qualitative and quantitative measures, coaches can gain a holistic view of the client's progress and areas needing improvement.

Tracking Progress

Regular tracking of progress is crucial to maintaining motivation and ensuring the effectiveness of the coaching program. This involves setting benchmarks and regularly reviewing progress against these benchmarks. Technology can play a significant role here, with apps and digital tools providing real-time feedback and facilitating continuous monitoring.

Feedback and Adaptation

Feedback is a vital component of the evaluation process. It allows clients to understand their progress and areas where they need to focus more. Moreover, feedback should be a two-way street, with clients also providing input on the coaching process itself. This helps in refining and adapting coaching strategies to better meet the client's needs.

Continuous Improvement

Effective health coaching is an ongoing process of evaluation, feedback, and adaptation. By continuously assessing the client's progress and adjusting the coaching strategies accordingly, health coaches can help clients achieve sustainable improvements in their health and well-being. This dynamic and responsive approach ensures that the coaching remains relevant and effective, tailored to the evolving needs of the client.

In summary, evaluation and assessment in health coaching are integral to achieving successful outcomes. By employing a structured and flexible approach to evaluation, health coaches can better support their clients on their journey to improved health and well-being.

CHAPTER 10

Building a Successful Health Coaching Practice

Creating a business, at its core, is an attempt to improve one's life through a venture that is personally meaningful. As a health coach, this business is centered on the importance of physical, mental, and emotional balance. To sustain a venture, it must generate enough revenue to cover costs. If it fails to do so, a payroll job will likely take priority. Business development is the process of ensuring net profit. It typically follows five stages outlined here as they specifically apply to health coaching:

Marketing and Client Retention

Marketing and client retention are mandatory in developing a clientele. Consistently engage in both to attract new clients. Marketing, or community service, refers to spreading a message that attracts people who may be interested in your coaching services. This message typically introduces the concept of health coaching, its principles, and the benefits. Networking goes hand in hand with marketing, as meeting new people and treating them as prospects is crucial. Once identified as a prospect, assess their sincerity in wanting to improve, and thus their potential to become a client. This is done through pre-enrollment, detailed in Section C of our Marketing Course.

Client retention refers to keeping clients engaged during their coaching period. Use daily action responses and periodic satisfaction surveys to maintain engagement. Offer special events and celebrations at various intervals throughout the year. Hold long-term "stick to living" guidance-based events monthly. Retained clients provide referrals as a natural byproduct, beginning the cycle anew as satisfied clients refer friends to experience your services. At Myers Detox, we target retaining over 90% of clients annually.

Business Development and Marketing

One objective of health coaching is to create an ongoing and consistent stream of clientele for your business. Previous chapters have detailed the best ways to create and manage a health coaching relationship. You may also wish to provide additional group coaching, classes, and seminars. Here, we will explore the features of running a successful health coaching business, including creating and maintaining a clientele, securing venues and guest speakers, and pricing coaching sessions and programs.

Business Development: There are many coaching businesses; distinguishing yours and marketing it successfully is crucial. Be clear about your niche market, your ideal client, and how to connect with this person. Advocating for your client base can be as simple as identifying patterns in your own client list, making calls, or polling potential clients. Once you have a client base, building from referrals is the easiest way to expand.

If you wish to focus primarily on coaching and not on business operations, hire additional services for marketing. This can range from a virtual assistant to a national marketing campaign. Running seminars or retreats marketed to your target population is an excellent way to quickly build your clientele. Attendees will likely need and desire your services after the seminar or wellness getaway, providing additional revenue. Marketing seminars also require public and community speaking.

Client Retention Strategies

Techniques to keep those you worked hard to find: Some professionals may experience constant client turnover. However, patient research suggests that the best marketing tool is word of mouth from current clients. Retaining clients longer increases the likelihood of future clients through referrals.

Stay proactive. Don't wait for clients to lose interest in health coaching to reach out. Regular, consistent outreach can include follow-up phone calls after providing resources to show you care about their progress. It's imperative that these calls or emails come from YOU, not a front desk staff or secretary. Make the client feel valued with personal, direct communication. Former clients who stopped coming in can be great sources of referrals. Reach out and invite them back.

Help your clients stick around and continue seeing the benefits of working with you. The art of health coaching, bringing your professional theories and recommendations to clients in an understandable format, is essential for client retention.

Lastly, build a strong bridge and open communication with your clients to discuss follow-up care. Frame this follow-up care as FREE. Offer a 15-minute appointment a few weeks down the road at no cost. This highlights the need to return. Use this time for additional assessment and intervention, and discuss how many "check-in" visits would support their needs. Remember, cash-based care often prides itself on spending more time with patients. It's not just the quantity of time but the quality as well. The Medicare population, in particular, suffers due to intricate coding and less time for meaningful interaction.

By focusing on these strategies, health coaches can build a successful practice that not only attracts but also retains clients, ensuring sustained growth and impact.

CHAPTER 11

Continuing Education and Professional Development

Read on for professional tips and continuing education opportunities in: Nutrition, Habit Building, Obesity Care, Entrepreneurship, and more! Continuing your education isn't just an option; it's integral to your success in the industry. Professionals dedicated to the field integrate ongoing education into their weekly routines. We understand that as a health or wellness professional, it's not just about finding the right behavior but ensuring you have the skills and knowledge to better inform and support your clients.

As a health coach, counselor, or health and wellness professional, it is necessary to commit to self- and professional development. Consistently hone targeted skills in building rapport, behavior change, effective communication, and understanding how to individualize recommendations. Look for courses that are practical, specialized, and intensive in their ability to increase your "smarts."

In addition to the courses described above, we encourage you to seek continuing education opportunities online, in-person, in formalized settings, or through self-study that resonate with your personal and professional growth trajectory. Explore courses that expand upon the knowledge you already have and those that will allow you to become a leading provider within your sub-specialty. For example, a health coach with an integrative and functional medicine certification might attend a webinar or workshop exploring small intestine bacterial overgrowth or Lyme disease.

Continuous learning is essential for staying at the forefront of the health and wellness field. Embrace every opportunity to grow your expertise and deliver the best possible guidance and support to your clients.